A Little Irish Cookbook

John Murphy

ILLUSTRATED BY KAREN BAILEY

Chronicle

D0402947

First published in the United States 1986 by
Chronicle Books
One Hallidie Plaza
San Francisco. CA 94102

First published in Ireland by
The Appletree Press Ltd. 1986

9 8 7 6 5 4 3

ISBN 0 87701 400 0

Text © John Murphy. 1986

Illustrations © Karen Bailey. 1986

Printed in Ireland

Introduction

I make no claims that this small book will give the reader anything more than a taste of Ireland. I do not, and indeed cannot, pretend that it is a comprehensive collection of traditional Irish recipes nor do I attempt to define, if it were even possible, an Irish cuisine. All I say is that if a visitor to Ireland were to encounter only what is in this book during a short stay then he would be satisfied that he had eaten well in the Irish style.

A note on measures

In Ireland, Imperial measures — pounds, pints, etc. — are most widely used. However, metric measures —kilogrammes, litres, etc. — are now the order of the day in schools, and of course American readers will be more at home with cups and spoons. All three methods have been used in this book — but don't mix them. If you use pounds of flour don't use litres of liquid as you will upset the balance of the more critical ingredients. Generally the cup referred to is the standard American measure, and the spoonfuls are level, not heaped, unless stated otherwise. Where the quantity is not critical I have given only the cup measure as an indication. For example, a variation on soda bread calls for ½ cup of dried fruit. A little more or less, within reason, will do no harm, and the cup in this instance should be regarded as a convenient measure rather than a precise one.

Irish Farmhouse Breakfast

I have fond memories of a particularly sunny summer a year or two ago when I stayed in a farmhouse on the Dingle peninsula. As well as the good weather I remember the breakfasts.

Start off with a freshly-cut half grapefruit with a dusting of caster sugar, followed by a bowl of smooth porridge of oatmeal gently cooked in milk and served with an individual jug of cream. After that comes rashers, sausages and eggs, the lot served with scones and brown bread warm from the oven, honey, homemade preserves, fresh butter and a pot of tea.

For each person gently fry two sausages over a low heat until well cooked through and golden brown on the outside. Also fry a couple of slices each of black and white pudding. Remove from the pan and keep hot. Drain off the fat, as it is somewhat indigestible, and fry two rashers of bacon, having first cut off the rind. Now fry a couple of eggs in the bacon fat, spooning the hot fat over the yolks to set them. Fry a few mushrooms, half a tomato and a slice or two of potato cake each. Add a knob of butter if there is not sufficient bacon fat, but do not cook in butter alone as it burns at too low a temperature.

Soda Bread

This bread is popular throughout Ireland. Because it is easily and quickly made it is often baked fresh for tea or even breakfast. At home we used to call the loaf made with white flour soda bread, while that made with wholemeal was wheaten bread. In other parts of the country wheaten bread is referred to as brown soda or, confusingly, soda bread!

---

1 lb / ½ kg / 4 cups plain flour
1 tsp salt
1 tsp baking soda
1 tsp sugar (optional)
1 pt / ½ lr / 2 cups buttermilk or sour milk

Sieve the dry ingredients into a large bowl. Scoop up handfuls and allow to drop back into the bowl to aerate the mixture. Add enough buttermilk to make a soft dough. Now work quickly as the buttermilk and soda are already reacting. Knead the dough lightly — too much handling will toughen it, while too little means it won't rise properly.

Form a round loaf about as thick as your fist. Place it on a lightly-floured baking sheet and cut a cross in the top with a floured knife. Put at once to bake near the top of a pre-heated oven, gas mark 8, 450°F, 230°C, for 30-45 minutes. When baked, the loaf will sound hollow when rapped on the bottom with your knuckles. Wrap immediately in a clean tea-towel to stop the crust hardening too much.

Wheaten bread or **brown soda** is made in exactly the same way but with wholemeal flour replacing all or some of the white flour; this mixture will probably require less buttermilk. Another variation is to add ½ cup of sultanas to the white bread — this loaf is known as **Spotted Dick.**

A Pot of Tea

It is easy to make a poor cup of tea. Float a tea bag in some milk, pour in some nearly-boiling water, mash the tea bag against the side of the cup with a spoon, fish out the tea bag and throw it away. There you are. Awful!

Tea should be made with freshly-drawn, freshly-boiled water in a warmed pot and allowed to brew. The result will be a pleasant, refreshing drink. To make a good pot of tea, bring freshly-drawn water to a brisk boil. Pour a little into a 2 pt / 1 lr / 4 cup earthenware teapot to warm it, then empty the water out. Using good quality tea, put 3-5 teaspoons, according to taste, into the warmed pot. Bring the water back to the boil and pour on immediately. Cover the pot with a tea-cosy and allow to brew for 5 minutes — any shorter and the flavour will not have developed, any longer and the tannin will start to come out, making the tea taste stewed. For the same reason, boiling water should be used to make the tea but the brew should not subsequently be boiled.

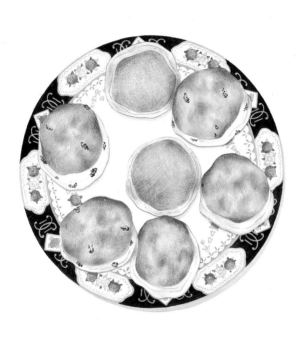

Scones

8 oz / 250 g / 2 cups self-raising flour
1 1/2 oz / 50 g / 3 tbsp butter
1/4 pt / 150 ml / 1/2 cup milk
pinch of salt

Sieve the flour into a bowl and rub in the butter quickly and lightly with the fingertips. Add the salt and then, using a round-bladed knife, mix in the milk a little at a time. With floured hands knead lightly to a soft dough, adding a little more milk if necessary. Roll out evenly but lightly about one finger thick on a floured board. Cut out with a pastry cutter using a quick sharp motion, but do not twist or the scones will distort as they bake. Cook on a greased baking sheet near the top of a pre-heated oven at gas mark 7, 425°F, 220°C for 12-15 mins.

These scones are best baked fresh for tea as they go stale very quickly. **Brown scones** are made in exactly the same way, substituting wholemeal flour for half the white flour. For **fruit scones** add a tablespoonful of caster sugar and two tablespoonfuls of dried fruit before adding the milk.

Apple Jelly

This well-flavoured jelly is very easy to make and will keep — if given a chance. It is delicious on hot, buttered scones or pancakes. The secret lies in the long, slow cooking which extracts the maximum amount of pectin — the setting agent — from the fruit. To ensure a clear, bright jelly it is vital to resist manfully the temptation to squeeze the pulp when straining the liquid.

---

5 lb/2 kg apples
12 whole cloves
4 pt/2 lr/8 cups water
4 lb/2 kg/8 cups sugar

Wash and quarter the apples. There is no need to peel or core them. Place in an ovenproof dish and add water. Cover, with aluminium foil if necessary. Cook overnight at the bottom of the oven, gas mark ½, 225°F, 110°C. Next day strain through a jelly bag or a clean, white pillow case — do not squeeze! Measure the liquid into a large saucepan and for every cupful add a cupful of sugar. Heat to dissolve the sugar and bring to the boil for about 10 minutes or until a little of the mixture gels on a cold saucer. Be careful here, as over-boiling will produce a syrup which will just get thicker without setting. Pour into jars which have been warmed in the oven and cover with waxed discs and lids.

Barm Brack

1/4 pt/125 ml/1/2 cup lukewarm milk	1 egg
1 tsp sugar	3 tbsp butter
1 tsp fresh yeast	6 oz/200 g/2 cups mixed fruit (currants, sultanas, raisins, candied peel)
8 oz/250 g/2 cups plain flour	
1 tsp mixed spice	2 oz/50 g/2 tbsp caster sugar
pinch salt	

Cream the yeast and the sugar and allow to froth up in the milk, which should be at blood heat. Sieve the flour, caster sugar and spice and rub in the butter. Make a well in the centre and add the yeast mixture and the egg, beaten. Beat with a wooden spoon for about 10 minutes until a good dough forms. The fruit and the salt should be worked in by hand and the whole kneaded. Put in a warm bowl, cover and allow to rise in a warm place for about an hour until doubled in size.

Knead lightly and place in a lightly-greased 7 in/15 cm diameter cake tin and allow a further 30 minutes rising time. Bake near the top of a pre-heated oven at gas mark 6, 400°F, 200°C for 45 minutes. On removing from the oven the brack can be glazed with a syrup made from 2 tsp sugar dissolved in 3 tsp boiling water.

Drop Scones · Pancakes

These are also known as Scotch Pancakes, especially in the north. They must be cooked as soon as possible after mixing, as the acid in the buttermilk starts to react with the baking soda at once. For that reason the griddle or pan should be heated before combining the ingredients.

---

8 oz / 250 g / 2 cups plain flour
$\frac{1}{2}$ tsp baking soda
$\frac{1}{2}$ tsp salt 1 tsp sugar 1 large egg
$\frac{1}{2}$ pt / 250 ml / 1 cup buttermilk

Sift the dry ingredients into a bowl. Make a well in the middle with a wooden spoon and add the egg. Break the yolk and pour in the buttermilk, mixing quickly to a thick batter. Do not beat, as this would develop the gluten in the flour and prevent the pancakes from rising. Fry in large dollops on a lightly-greased, hot griddle or heavy frying pan. Drop scones are best served hot for tea, thickly spread with melting butter and syrup or jam.

Here is an easy way to make thin pancakes:

---

4 oz / 125 g / 1 cup plain flour
pinch salt · 2 eggs
$\frac{1}{2}$ pt / 250 ml / 1 cup milk
1 tbsp melted butter

Put all the ingredients in a blender and blend for about 30 seconds. The batter should then be allowed to stand for

30 minutes in a cool place. Heat a small pan over a medium heat. Grease with a little butter and wipe out with kitchen paper. Fry about 2 tbsp of batter at a time, swirling to cover the base of the pan. Keep them thin and there will be no need to turn. Serve rolled up with sugar.

Potato Farls

Also known as potato cake or potato bread, this is very much a northern dish. It is an important — indeed essential — constituent of the Ulster Fry, alongside bacon, egg, sausage and perhaps fried soda farl.

The recipe calls for cooked, mashed potatoes. These should be freshly boiled, or, better still, steamed and passed through a food mill, and used warm.

---

2 lb/1 kg/2 cups mashed potatoes
4 oz/125 g/1 cup plain flour
2 tbsp butter
salt

Melt the butter and mix into the potatoes with the salt. Work in the flour quickly but thoroughly and knead lightly. Divide in two and roll out each half on a floured board to form a circle about the size of a large dinner plate. Cut in quarters (farls) and cook for about 3 minutes on each side in a heavy frying pan in a little bacon fat.

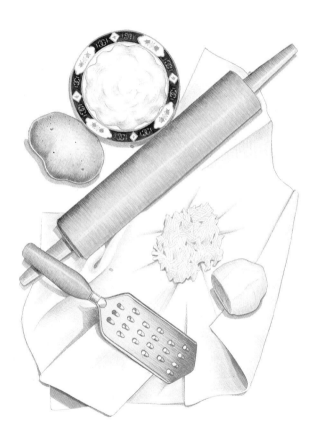

Boxty

Boxty is a traditional potato dish, celebrated in the rhyme:

Boxty on the griddle, boxty in the pan,
If you can't make boxty, you'll never get your man.

---

8 oz/250 g/1 cup raw potato
8 oz/250 g/1 cup mashed potato
8 oz/250 g/2 cups plain flour
1 tsp baking powder
1 tsp salt
large knob of butter, melted
about ¼ pt/125 ml/½ cup milk

Grate the raw potatoes into a bowl. Turn out onto a cloth and wring, catching the liquid. This will separate into a clear fluid with starch at the bottom. Pour off the fluid and scrape out the starch and mix with the grated and mashed potatoes. Sieve the dry ingredients and mix in along with the melted butter. Add a little milk if necessary to make a pliable dough. Knead lightly on a floured surface. Divide into four and form large, flat cakes. Mark each into quarters but do not cut right through, and bake on a griddle or in a heavy pan.

If liked, more milk and an egg can be added to make a batter which can be fried in bacon fat like drop scones (see recipe, p. 17).

Dulse and Yellowman

Did you treat your Mary Ann to dulse and yellowman
At the Ould Lammas Fair at Ballycastle-O?

Dulse is a purple, edible seaweed. I remember buying it at
a penny a bag as a child when sweets were hard to get. It
can also be stewed for a couple of hours and eaten as a
vegetable or with oatcakes. It is not known much outside
the north of Ireland — and it is no great loss!
  Yellowman is a different matter altogether. This tooth-
some, honeycombed, sticky toffee is traditionally sold at
the Ould Lammas Fair at the end of August.

---

1 lb/½ kg/1½ cups golden or corn syrup
8 oz/250 g/1 cup brown sugar
1 tbsp butter (heaped)
2 tbsp vinegar
1 tsp baking soda

In a large saucepan slowly melt together all the ingredients
except the baking soda. Do not stir. Boil until a drop
hardens in cold water (240°F, 190°C on a sugar
thermometer). Stir in the baking soda. The toffee will
immediately foam up as the vinegar releases the gas from
the baking soda. Pour out onto a greased slab and while
just cool enough to handle fold the edges towards the
centre and pull repeatedly until the whole is a pale yellow
colour. Allow to cool and harden in a greased tin and
break into chunks with a toffee hammer — or anything
else that comes to hand.

Potato Soup

The basis of a good soup — especially a simple soup such as this — is a good stock. The soup should be made with a white stock, that is, water in which a chicken, ham or bacon has been boiled. Alternatively, stock can be made from a ham bone or a chicken carcass boiled with a few root vegetables and herbs as available, and an onion. The stock should be strained, allowed to cool and the fat removed from the surface.

---

6 medium potatoes
2 medium onions
3 pt/1 1/2 lr/6 cups stock or milk and water mixed
1 tbsp butter
parsley
salt and pepper
(serves six)

Peel and dice the potatoes and chop the onions. Melt the butter and gently cook the onions and potatoes in a covered saucepan until soft but not coloured. Add the liquid, adjust the seasoning to taste, sieve if wished and serve in bowls decorated with a little chopped parsley.

Pea and Ham Soup

This soup is made with dried peas; these generally have to be soaked overnight, though it is possible to buy some that need only a few hours' immersion. It is slightly less trouble to make the soup with split peas — which have no skins — and here there is a choice of green or yellow. Although there is no difference in the taste, the latter give the soup a pleasant golden colour.

---

1 lb / 500 g / 2 cups dried peas or split peas
4 oz / 125 g / 1/2 cup diced pieces of cooked ham or a ham bone
1 large onion and a little fat (optional)
3 pts / 1 1/2 lr / 6 cups ham stock or water
cream (optional)
parsley (optional)
seasoning
(serves six)

Soak the peas as directed on the packet. Chop the onion, if used, and soften in a little fat over a low heat. Add the peas and water or stock and the ham bone if used.

Cook gently until the peas are soft — about an hour. Remove the bone and strip off any meat. This should be cut into small dice and reserved. Puree the peas in a blender or pass through a sieve. Adjust the seasoning. Add the diced ham and serve with a swirl of cream or a sprinkling of chopped parsley on top.

Mutton Broth

It is a good idea to make this broth a day in advance. The fat that rises to the surface will solidify and can easily be removed.

---

2 lb / 1 kg neck of mutton
3 pt / 2 lr / 6 cups water
2 tbsp pearl barley
1 large onion
1 medium turnip
2 large carrots
1/2 small white cabbage
(serves six)

Put the meat in a large pan and cover with the cold water. Bring to the boil and skim the surface. Rinse the barley and add to the pan. Cover, but not too tightly, and simmer gently for 90 minutes. Shred the cabbage and dice the other vegetables and add these to the soup. Bring back to the boil and simmer for another hour. Remove the mutton and separate the meat from any bones, fat or gristle. Chop the meat and return to the soup. Allow to cool and remove fat. Reheat and serve.

Baked Salmon

There is no doubt that this is an expensive dish, but it will feed eight to ten people and makes a fine party piece.

---

1 whole fresh salmon (about 5 lb / 2 kg)
parsley
salt and pepper
1/2 cup butter
1/2 cup dry cider
1/2 pt / 250 ml / 1 cup double cream
(serves eight to ten)

Clean and descale the salmon, cut off the head and tail and trim the fins. Stuff the parsley into the gullet. Butter some aluminium foil and form a loose envelope round the fish, sealing both ends but leaving the top open for the moment. Dot the rest of the butter over the salmon, season and pour over the cider and the cream. Now seal the foil along the top, leaving only a small vent. Bake in the oven for 1¼ hours at gas mark 4, 350°F, 180°C. When ready, take from the oven, remove the skin and reduce the sauce by boiling, stirring all the time. Serve with boiled new potatoes and fresh garden peas.

Dublin Lawyer

This dish is delicious and traditional — a happy combination — though its expensive ingredients make it a rare treat rather than an everyday affair. For the best flavour the fish has to be freshly killed just before cooking. Plunge a sharp knife into the cross on the back of the head. Slice in half lengthwise and crack open the claws. Remove all the flesh and cut into large chunks. Keep both halves of the shell for serving.

---

1 live lobster, about 2 lb/1 kg
4 oz/125 g/½ cup butter
½ cup Irish whiskey
¼ pt/150 ml/½ cup whipping cream
salt and pepper
(serves two)

Toss the lobster meat in foaming butter over a medium heat for a few minutes until cooked. Take care that the butter does not burn. Add the whiskey and when it has heated up set light to it. Pour in the cream, heat through and season. Serve in the half shells with plainly boiled fine beans.

Champ

Champ is a simple, warming dish which is cheap, easy to produce and very filling. When I was a child we used to have it at Hallowe'en for dinner. A silver sixpenny piece wrapped in greaseproof paper would be buried in it. To find it in your portion was to bring good luck for a year —quite apart from the temporary wealth.

8 medium potatoes, peeled
small bunch of scallions (spring onions)
1/4 pt / 125 ml / 1/2 cup milk
salt and pepper
knob of butter per person
(serves four)

The best way to prepare the potatoes is to cook them in a steamer and then pass them through a food mill. Alternatively, boil until soft but not mushy, drain and return them to the heat to dry somewhat before mashing. In any case keep hot. Chop the scallions finely, both green and white parts, and cook for 5 minutes in the milk. Beat this mixture into the mashed potatoes until smooth and fluffy, season to taste and serve a large mound on each plate with a good knob of butter melting into the top. Each forkful is dipped into the the melted butter as it is eaten. Very good with a glass of cold milk.

Colcannon is made in much the same way as Champ, but with the addition of cabbage. In parts of the country white cabbage is always used. In any case, shred and chop a small cabbage (discard the stump) and cook until tender. Beat into the potato mixture and serve as above.

Spiced Beef

Spiced beef is traditionally eaten at Christmas time. It tends to be rather expensive to buy as it is quite labour intensive to make, though it uses a modestly enough priced cut. It can be made at home, but it does take time.

7 lb / 3 kg even-sized piece of topside or silverside	2 tbsp black treacle
2 tsp each ground cloves, milled black pepper, allspice, cinnamon, mace and saltpetre	2 tbsp brown sugar
	cold water to cover
	bottle Guinness
	1/2 cup salt

Combine all the ingredients except the beef, water and Guinness. Place the beef in a bowl and cover with the mixture. Rub it in once or twice a day for a week. Tie up the meat into a good shape and place in a pan. Cover with cold water to which a bottle of Guinness has been added. Simmer gently for 5-6 hours. When cool, press lightly between two plates. The beef is usually served cold, thinly sliced.

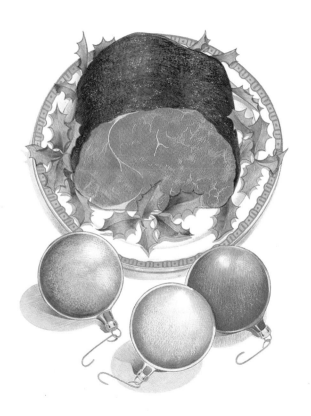

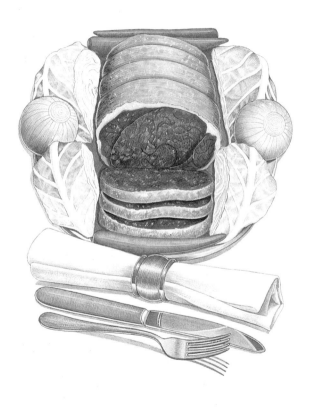

Corned Beef and Cabbage

Corned beef is brisket, topside or silverside which has been pickled in brine. It is especially popular around Dublin. It is best to soak a joint overnight to remove excess salt.

---

5 lb / 2 kg joint of corned beef	1 large cabbage
2 large onions	bay leaf
2 large carrots	cold water to cover
4 potatoes	ground black pepper

(serves four to six)

Quarter the cabbage and put aside. Peel and slice the other vegetables. Cover the meat with the water and bring to the boil. Skim the surface, add the vegetables (except the cabbage), the bay leaf and the pepper and simmer gently for 90 minutes. Add the cabbage and cook for a further 30 minutes. Serve the meat surrounded by the vegetables with additional mashed potatoes.

Baked Limerick Ham

To the Irish, ham is a cured leg of pork. The preserving process is carried out in a number of different ways: salting, smoking, immersion in brine or even honey. Traditionally, Limerick ham is smoked over juniper branches. Whole hams should be steeped in cold water overnight before cooking but this is not necessary with smaller joints. The ham in this recipe is not really baked but rather finished off in the oven after having been cooked by simmering in cider.

3-5 lb/1½-2 kg ham
cider to cover
½ cup brown sugar
1 tsp mustard
20 whole cloves

Cover the ham with cold water and bring slowly to the boil. Throw out the water and replace with cider. Bring this just to the boil and lower the heat, keeping the liquid barely simmering for 20 minutes to the 1 lb/½ kg. Remove from the heat and allow to stand in the liquid for 30 minutes. Take out the ham, skin it and score the fat with a sharp knife in a diamond pattern. Stud with whole cloves. Mix the sugar and mustard and rub well into the surface of the ham. Bake in a pre-heated oven for a further 10 minutes to the 1 lb/½ kg at gas mark 6, 400°F, 200°C.

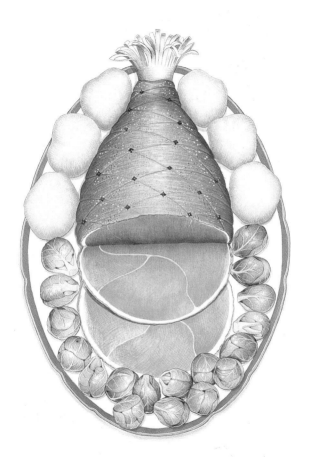

Beef in Guinness

The Guinness in this recipe has the same function as the wine in Coq Au Vin — the acid and moisture combined with the long, slow cooking help tenderise the tough but flavoursome meat.

2½ lb / 1 kg shin of beef
2 large onions
6 medium carrots
2 tbsp seasoned flour
a little fat or beef dripping
½ pt / 250 ml / 1 cup Guinness and water mixed
sprig of parsley
(serves four)

Cut the beef into chunks and peel and slice the onions and carrots. Toss the beef in the flour and brown quickly in hot fat. Remove the beef and fry the onions gently until transparent. Return the beef and add the carrots and the liquid. Bring just to the boil, reduce the heat to a very gentle simmer, cover closely and cook for 1½-2 hours. Check that the dish does not dry out, adding more liquid if necessary. Sprinkle with chopped parsley and serve with plainly boiled potatoes.

Irish Stew

Irish stew is easy to make and if made with mutton and cooked slowly will be both favoursome and tender. Mutton, being an older meat, has more flavour than lamb but does need to be cooked for a couple of hours over a low heat with liquid. It should not be allowed to boil or the flavour will be spoiled. There is little agreement as to the classic recipe — should there be carrots? Should the meat be browned? Should mutton, lamb, beef, bacon or even kid be used? The following dish will be found to be hearty and nourishing and traditional enough.

2½ lb / 1 kg boned mutton	sprig of parsley
4 large potatoes	1 pt / 500 ml / 2 cups water
2 large onions	salt and pepper
3 or 4 medium carrots	

(serves four)

Cut the meat into good sized chunks. Peel the vegetables and slice thickly. Chop the parsley. Choose a pot with a well-fitting lid and put in the ingredients in layers, starting and finishing with potatoes. Pour in the water and season to taste. Cover and put on a very low heat for about 2½ hours until the meat is tender and the potatoes have thickened the liquid. The dish may also be made with lamb, in which case it requires only 1½ hours cooking time.

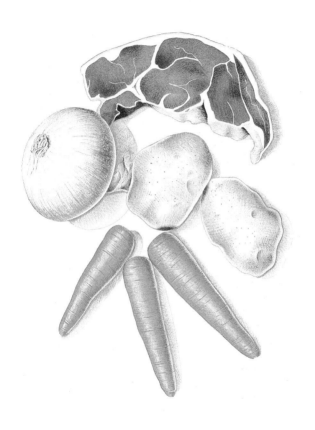

Dublin Coddle

This is a very popular dish, especially in Dublin, and has been so for many years. It is nourishing, tasty, economical and warming — what more could you ask? Although it is best made with a good stock — water in which a ham has been boiled, perhaps, or even a ham bone — a light stock cube will substitute.

---

1 lb/500 g best sausages
8 oz/250 g streaky bacon
1/2 pt/300 ml/1 cup stock or water
6 medium potatoes
2 medium onions
salt and pepper
(serves four)

Cut the bacon into 1 in/3 cm squares. Bring the stock to the boil in a medium saucepan which has a well-fitting lid, add the sausages and the bacon and simmer for about 5 minutes. Remove the sausages and bacon and save the liquid. Cut each sausage into four or five pieces. Peel the potatoes and cut into thick slices. Skin the onions and slice them. Assemble a layer of potatoes in the saucepan, followed by a layer of onions and then half the sausages and bacon. Repeat the process once more and then finish off with a layer of potatoes. Pour the reserved stock over and season lightly to taste. Cover and simmer gently for about an hour. Adjust the seasoning and serve piping hot.

Blackberry Sorbet

A fresh fruit sorbet is a delightfully refreshing culmination to any meal. As a method of preserving the taste of a warm autumn into the depths of winter this simply-made sorbet is second to none. From late August to mid-October wild blackberries can be picked from bushes by the side of country roads throughout Ireland. A wet summer followed by a warm, dry autumn will ensure a bumper crop.

---

1 lb/500 g/2 cups fresh blackberries
4 oz/125 g/½ cup sugar
¼ pt/125 ml/½ cup water
2 egg whites
(serves four)

Clean the blackberries thoroughly and remove stalks. Liquidise the fruit in a blender and strain through a sieve. Dissolve the sugar in the water and boil for about 5 minutes to make a syrup. Add the blackberries and boil for a further minute. When the liquid has cooled, fold it into stiffly-beaten egg whites. Freeze in an ice-cream machine or in ice cube trays in the freezer compartment of a fridge. If the latter is used, the mixture should be stirred about once an hour to prevent large ice crystals developing.

Rhubarb Fool

A fruit fool is a simple and delicious dessert, rich and creamy — but not overly so.

6-8 plump sticks of rhubarb
4 oz / 25 g / ½ cup sugar
small knob butter
½ pt / 250 ml / 1 cup whipping cream
(serves four)

Cut the rhubarb into chunks and sweat with the sugar and butter over a low heat until cooked but not mushy. Liquidise or pass through a food mill. When cold, fold into stiffly-whipped cream. Allow to set in a fridge and serve with Lady finger or Boudoir biscuits.

Apple or **gooseberry fool** is made in exactly the same way, except that in the case of gooseberries the puree should be sieved to remove pips. It may be necessary to adjust sugar to taste.

Gooseberry Crumble

This dish is an easily prepared and economical dessert, especially at the time of year when gooseberries are plentiful. The basic method can be used for other fillings, such as rhubarb, apple or apple and blackberry.

---

8 oz/250 g/2 cups self-raising flour
4 oz/125 g/½ cup soft brown sugar
4 oz/125 g/½ cup butter
2 lb/1 kg/10 cups gooseberries
6 oz/200 g/1 cup caster sugar

Using your fingertips, rub in the butter lightly into the flour in a large bowl. When it is like fine breadcrumbs mix in the brown sugar. Top and tail the berries and cover with the crumble mixture in an oven-proof dish, pressing the surface down lightly. Bake for 45 minutes in the centre of a pre-heated oven at gas mark 4, 350°F, 180°C. Serve hot with cream.

Apple Tart

The fat in the pastry for this pie should be half butter and half lard as this gives a good flavour; however, all butter may be used if wished. A light touch when rubbing in is essential and everything should be kept cool. The pastry should be allowed to 'rest' for half an hour in a cool place before rolling out.

Pastry	Filling
8 oz/250 g/2 cups plain flour	4 or 5 medium cooking apples
4 oz/125 g/½ cup fat	2 tbsp brown sugar
pinch salt	3 or 4 cloves (optional)
iced water	

Rub the cold fat into the sieved flour in a large bowl. When it looks like fine breadcrumbs add two or three tablespoonfuls of iced water to bind, mixing with a round-bladed knife. Knead lightly and allow to rest before rolling out. Line a 9 inch/25 cm metal pie dish with half the pastry. Peel and thinly slice the apples and put on the pastry base. Sprinkle the sugar over. Roll out the rest of the pastry as a lid, dampening the base around the edge to help it stick. Cut a vent in the top and bake near the top of the oven for 30 minutes at gas mark 7, 425°F, 220°C. Serve hot or cold with cream.

Porter Cake

Porter is a type of dark Irish beer, not now as widely available as it once was. It is not as strong as stout but Guinness, Murphy's or other Irish stout can be substituted in this recipe if mixed fifty-fifty with water. This cake is quickly and easily made and, though it tastes good fresh from the oven, it is best kept for about a week in an airtight tin.

½ pt / 250 ml / 1 cup porter
8 oz / 250 g / 1 cup butter
8 oz / 250 g / 1 cup brown sugar
2 lb / 1 kg / 6 cups mixed dried fruit (equal quantities currants, raisins, sultanas with about half as much mixed peel)

1¼ lb / ½ kg / 4 cups plain flour
½ tsp baking soda
1 tsp mixed spice
grated rind from one small lemon (optional)
3 medium eggs

Melt the butter and sugar in the porter in a saucepan. Add the fruit and simmer for 10 minutes. Allow to go cold and add the sieved flour, baking soda, spices and lemon rind. Beat the eggs and mix in with a wooden spoon. Pour into a greased and lined 9 inch / 25 cm cake tin and bake on the middle shelf of a pre-heated oven at gas mark 3, 325°F, 160°C for about 1¾ hours. To test the cake, push a skewer into the centre; if ready, the skewer will come out clean. Allow the cake to cool in the tin.

Irish Coffee · Hot Whiskey

¾ cup hot, strong, black coffee
1-2 tsp sugar
1 large measure Irish whiskey
1-2 tbsp double cream

Fill a stemmed whiskey glass with hot water then throw out, refilling it with boiling water. Throw this out, fill the glass somewhat more than half full with coffee and add sugar to taste. Stir to dissolve, then add the whiskey. Pour the cream over the back of a spoon to float on top.

Drink the hot liquid through the cool cream. If double cream is not available use lightly-whipped single (whipping) cream.

Hot Whiskey, also known as 'hot Irish' or just 'punch', is a favourite winter drink in Irish pubs.

boiling water
1-2 tsp sugar
1 large measure Irish whiskey
slice of lemon
2 or 3 whole cloves

Heat a stemmed whiskey glass as above. Pour in fresh boiling water to more than half full, dissolve sugar to taste, add the whiskey, a slice of lemon and the cloves. Serve at once.

Index

Apple Crumble 52
Apple and Blackberry Crumble 52
Apple Fool 51
Apple Jelly 12
Apple Tart 55

Baked Limerick Ham 40
Baked Salmon 31
Barm Brack 14
Beef in Guinness 43
Blackberry Sorbet 48
Boxty 21
Breakfast, Irish Farmhouse 4
Brown Scones 11
Brown Soda 8
Buttermilk Pancakes see Drop
    Scones

Champ 35
Coddle 47
Coffee, Irish 58
Colcannon 35
Corned Beef and Cabbage 39

Drop Scones 17
Dublin Lawyer 32
Dulse 22

Fruit Scones 11

Gooseberry Crumble 52
Gooseberry Fool 51

Ham, Baked Limerick 40

Hot Whiskey 58
Irish Coffee 58
Irish Farmhouse Breakfast 4
Irish Stew 44

Lobster see Dublin Lawyer

Mutton Broth 29

Pancakes 17
Pea and Ham Soup 26
Porter Cake 57
Potato Farls 18
Potato Soup 25

Rhubarb Crumble 52
Rhubarb Fool 51

Salmon, Baked 31
Scones 11
Scotch Pancakes see Drop
    Scones
Soda Bread 7
Spiced Beef 36
Spotted Dick 8

Tea 8

Wheaten Bread 8
Whiskey, Hot 58

Yellowman 22